"This in-depth study carries the timeless truth of the incredible v
their significance in the message of the gospel. Within these page:
highlighting the eternal truth that the Word of God is inspiring and alive. The rich theology will equip
you with vital 'information,' while the reflection and meditation questions will take you on a journey
of 'transformation.'"

JULIE MULLINS, senior pastor, Christ Fellowship, Florida

"Marina Hofman, PhD, is a lover of God, of truth, of knowledge and understanding, and of people.
She cares deeply about equipping people in their full identity available through God in Christ, and
especially on behalf of women. Hofman is a gift to the world and to all who hunger for deeper
knowledge of the truth that sets us free."

**COLONEL JANET MUNN, DMin, director of The Salvation Army International Social Justice
Commission**

"The Bible testifies that women have played, and will continue to play, an essential role in God's loving
plan of salvation. Marina Hofman's Bible study makes accessible to Christians of all denominations,
and indeed to all searchers after truth, a way of growing in appreciation of that important truth
through an insightful small group Bible sharing format. As a Catholic priest and a Missionary of
Mercy, I especially enjoy Marina's engaging invitation to meditate on the role that Mary plays in God's
plan."

FATHER BILL TRUSZ, parish priest and Missionary of Mercy

"Marina Hofman is the Bible teacher and spiritual mentor we all wish we had. *Women in the Bible*
provides a fresh approach by this seasoned disciple-maker to unlock the scriptural truths of our
spiritual mothers. I believe every woman who gathers a few friends and dives into this study will be
encouraged, inspired, and transformed."

**KADI COLE, leadership consultant, executive coach, and author of *Developing Female Leaders* and
Find Your Leadership Voice in 90 Days (www.kadicole.com)**

"This much needed Bible study series opens up the stories of women in the Bible in new and life-giving ways. Hofman's skills as a careful reader of Scripture stand behind her analysis of each character. Her probing questions push us to think about the significance of the stories of our biblical foremothers for our lives today. This book will be a very helpful resource for small group studies within the church."

MARION TAYLOR, PhD, Old Testament professor, Wycliffe College, University of Toronto

"This beautifully written Bible study on women in the Bible is inspirational, insightful, and practical. Hofman begins each study by raising relevant and meaningful questions that aid the reader in making careful observations on the biblical text. These interpretive questions are followed by a well-crafted and thoughtful reflection section that is both insightful and practical. She concludes each study with meditative prayers as a heartfelt response to the story. Hofman does not shy away from raising challenging questions regarding ambiguities and ethical dilemmas seen in some of the narratives, regarding deception, oppression, and injustices, and how the women navigate such difficult challenges. Hofman's perceptive conclusions about the women's courage and faith in the face of incredible obstacles and suffering are profound and relevant. Her study demonstrates well how these biblical stories contain life-affirming and hope-filled messages for us today. Readers of this Bible study will discover many gems, inspiring hope, faith, and encouragement."

REBECCA G. S. IDESTROM, PhD, associate professor of Old Testament, Tyndale Seminary of Tyndale University

"Hofman offers a Bible study for women that creates meaningful encounters with women in the Bible whom she presents as dynamic leaders. Through insightful questions, she creates a living experience of stories that encourage us and provide life patterns. We are encouraged by women seeing God coming through in the midst of challenging situations, overcoming obstacles and challenges, and experiencing blessing. We find models for taking risky or bold action, showing self-sacrificial love, waiting patiently for God to answer prayer, influencing and leading people, and being Christ to others."

CYNTHIA LONG WESTFALL, PhD, associate professor of New Testament, McMaster Divinity College, and author of *Paul and Gender*

"I thank God for giving me the opportunity to meet a woman who has blessed and edified my life. Marina Hofman is a woman with firm convictions in God and has put forth her life, abilities, gifts, and talents for the edification of others.

She is a woman who, by her call to serve and share what has been entrusted to her, was the first professor to share at the A.B. Simpson Missionary Training Center, regardless of the language and conditions that were lacking at the early stages. She is a woman dedicated to the service of others to plant seeds that have grown into the life of the call of missionaries.

As well, Marina was the first conference speaker at the first Impact of Women, giving the talk on 'How to be a Woman of Influence and Transcendence,' a sermon that left a mark on the lives of the women who had the privilege of attending and listening. That's why I think God has called her and she has responded to the call to be an instrument in God's hands and that has opened the way for others to be blessed. I thank Marina for her friendship and willingness to serve God and others.

I truly believe *Women in the Bible Small Group Bible Study* is an incredible resource for women all throughout the Americas and beyond! I can't wait to see what's to come as a result of this project! With love, gratitude, and admiration."

SONIA SANCHEZ, senior pastor and director for female pastors, Christian and Missionary Alliance, Colombia, South America

WOMEN
IN THE BIBLE
Small group Bible study

MARINA HOFMAN PhD

Published by Castle Quay Books
Burlington, Ontario, Canada and Jupiter, Florida, U.S.A.
416-573-3249 | info@castlequaybooks.com | www.castlequaybooks.com

The author acknowledges family, friends, and colleagues who invested time and expertise by providing feedback. Thank you.

Connect with the Marina through the website

www.womeninthebible.info

and **follow @marinahofman**

Library and Archives Canada Cataloguing in Publication Data
Title: Women in the Bible Small Group Bible Study
Names: Hofman, Marina H., 1981- author.
Identifiers: Canadiana 20200414860 | ISBN 9781988928432 (soft cover)
Subjects: LCSH: Women in the Bible.
Classification: LCC BS575 .H64 2021 | DDC 220.9/2082—dc23

978-1-988928-43-2 soft cover
978-1-988928-44-9 e-book

Contents

INTRODUCTORY NOTE

I am so excited that you are about to embark on a journey into God's word—and especially that you've chosen to study the women of the Bible! What a group of dynamic leaders, who have so much to teach us!

Here are eight Bible stories that can be studied in one setting or divided into two or three sessions each. Many women use this resource for personal devotional study; others journey through the chapters together in small groups. There is no homework or preparation required.

Free supplemental videos on each chapter are available at www.womeninthebible.info. These videos are short clips where I introduce the Bible passage and share how I personally connect to each woman's story. You are invited to freely use these videos in your sessions!

Please visit www.womeninthebible.info to connect with me and for all resources and information related to this study.

Thank you so much for investing your time in studying women in the Bible and bringing alongside other women on your journey!

Yours in Christ,

Marina

TO ACCESS THE FREE VIDEO SERIES
AND OTHER RESOURCES VISIT
WWW.WOMENINTHEBIBLE.INFO

Sarah and Hagar
GENESIS 16

Share a time when God came through for you or you sensed God's presence in the midst of a difficult or challenging situation.

BACKGROUND

God promised Abraham that he would have a child. As years passed, there was increased pressure on his wife, Sarah, to conceive. In time, Abraham expressed doubt about God's promise: "Sovereign LORD, what can you give me since I remain childless and the one who will inherit my estate is Eliezer of Damascus? … You have given me no children; so a servant in my household will be my heir."

But the LORD renewed the promise of a child to Abraham: "This man will not be your heir, but a son who is your own flesh and blood will be your heir" (Gen 15:2–4).

Sometime after this promise was given to Abraham (then called Abram), Sarah (then called Sarai) came to accept her infertility. She then tried to have a child through a surrogate.
So begins our story …

GENESIS

16 ¹ Now Sarai, Abram's wife, had borne him no children. But she had an Egyptian slave named Hagar; ² so she said to Abram, "The LORD has kept me from having children. Go, sleep with my slave; perhaps I can build a family through her." Abram agreed to what Sarai said.

³ So after Abram had been living in Canaan ten years, Sarai his wife took her Egyptian slave Hagar and gave her to her husband to be his wife. ⁴ He slept with Hagar, and she conceived. When she knew she was pregnant, she began to despise her mistress.

⁵ Then Sarai said to Abram, "You are responsible for the wrong I am suffering. I put my slave in your arms, and now that she knows she is pregnant, she despises me. May the LORD judge between you and me."

EXPLORE

16:1–2 Sarah and Abraham do not use Hagar's name; rather, we learn of her name from the narrator. Observe the titles used to refer to Hagar as the story progresses.

How does Sarah's statement show her faith?

16:3–4 It seems that there is a sense of resolution—a child for Sarah—but how do Hagar's actions indicate that things will not go as Sarah planned?

How does Hagar wrong Sarah?

16:5 Did Abraham indeed bear some responsibility?

6 "Your slave is in your hands," Abram said. "Do with her whatever you think best." Then Sarai mistreated Hagar; so she fled from her.

16:6 "Mistreated" could be translated "abused," as it means elsewhere in the Old Testament. How do Sarah's actions correspond with Abraham's instruction to do "whatever you think best"?

What does Hagar's response to flee from Sarah tell us about how Hagar is feeling?

7 The angel of the LORD found Hagar near a spring in the desert; it was the spring that is beside the road to Shur. 8 And he said, "Hagar, slave of Sarai, where have you come from, and where are you going?" "I'm running away from my mistress Sarai," she answered.

16:7–8 What do you make of this beautiful encounter with the angel so far?

Is it significant that the angel's first word identifies Hagar by name?

Does Hagar's response to the angel indicate that she is without a plan?

9 Then the angel of the LORD told her, "Go back to your mistress and submit to her." 10 The angel added, "I will increase your descendants so much that they will be too numerous to count." 11 The angel of the LORD also said to her: "You are now pregnant and you will give birth to a son. You shall name him Ishmael, for the LORD has heard of your misery. 12 He will be a wild donkey of a man; his hand will be against everyone and everyone's hand against him, and he will live in hostility toward all his brothers."

16:9–12 In her present situation, Hagar faces great danger—pregnant and alone in the wilderness with no provision or protection from wild animals and other travelers. Still, does the angel's instruction seem jarring?

Observe how the rest of the passage provides further context for the angel's words.

[13] She gave this name to the LORD who spoke to her: "You are the God who sees me," for she said, "I have now seen the One who sees me."

16:13 Hagar realizes that the "angel" is the LORD, and she is the only character in the Old Testament to give a name to the LORD!

How do you think this encounter impacts Hagar's self-worth and identity?

Does Hagar return to Sarah as the "same" person?

Do you think the divine promise for her son changes Hagar's outlook on the future?

[14] That is why the well was called Beer Lahai Roi; it is still there, between Kadesh and Bered.

16:14 The community commemorates Hagar's encounter by naming a well. How did they know Hagar's story?

Is there any indication that Hagar was further mistreated?

Is it possible that Hagar returns "seen" and protected by the community?

¹⁵ So Hagar bore Abram a son, and Abram gave the name Ishmael to the son she had borne.
¹⁶ Abram was eighty-six years old when Hagar bore him Ishmael.

16:15–16 How does Abraham know to call the child Ishmael?

Compare the characters listed at the end of the story with those in verse 1. Which character is this passage ultimately about?

DISCUSS

1. What does this story tell us about God's blessing?

2. What does Hagar's encounter with the angel reveal about God?

3. How can this story encourage those who are suffering?

4. What can we learn about how to respond to relationship tension and conflict?

REFLECTIONS

1. What does this story tell us about God's blessing?

Abraham and Sarah are blessed by God (as Genesis 12:2–3 indicates). But even though they are blessed, Abraham and Sarah face many trials. They endure years of infertility and surely wonder if they had heard correctly from God and if God is *able* to fulfill the promise of a child. Their lives exemplify that God's chosen ones are not exempt from suffering; a blessed person still experiences hardship. Some might say that there is a form of blessing in suffering—that suffering can cultivate a closeness to God, a deep commitment to faith. But it is not easy.

This passage demonstrates that God requires those who are blessed to act rightly toward others and to promote justice. God expects faithfulness and goodness. Sarah failed to treat Hagar as God expected, and Abraham failed to intervene on Hagar's behalf. As followers of Christ and as people blessed by God, we are called to be examples of Christlikeness to others. And when we see injustice, we are called to defend the cause of those who are disadvantaged.

The consequences of acting unjustly may be weighty. The events in this story present the beginning of a conflict between the lineages of Sarah (Israelites) and Hagar (Ishmaelites) that continued throughout the Old Testament. It can serve as a challenge to all of us to be peacemakers and to bear with one another in kindness and patience. How good to know that the Holy Spirit is present within us to guide us and help us.

2. What does Hagar's encounter with the angel reveal about God?

God sees *every* person. The promise God gives to Hagar about her son is much like the promise God gave to Abraham about his future offspring—this connection greatly elevates Hagar's standing in Genesis and reminds us that in God's kingdom, there is no "lowly" person unworthy of God's special blessing. There is no social status in God's kingdom; we are all children of God on equal standing. No person is undeserving of God's personal attention.

Whatever we are going through, God sees us in the midst of our situations and God is with us. Hagar surely faced hardships when she returned to Sarah; Genesis 21 confirms that the tension in the family was great and continued. When we face hardship, we can find encouragement in the story of Hagar. Just like the angel of the LORD finds Hagar in her darkest moment, on the run, so the LORD will come to us in our darkest moments.

We may actually sense God's presence strongest as we walk through our most difficult situations. As with Hagar, the LORD cares greatly for us, the LORD gives us a powerful sense of worth and identity, and the LORD bestows worth, value, and identity upon us.

3. How can this story encourage those who are suffering?

Sarah struggles with infertility despite God's promise of a child. Sarah's situation is further exacerbated by Hagar's response. As for Hagar, we are not told much about her. Was she forced to be with Abraham, or was she willing? Did she run away in complete desperation, or did she leave in confidence that she could start a new life on her own? One thing is for certain—Hagar was not in control over many aspects of her life.

We can relate to the trials of Sarah and Hagar. Many of us are familiar with the heartache of wanting a child and the agony associated with infertility. We have been in a position where we could not induce change or control the outcome of events.

So, we pray hard. But it becomes difficult to keep hopeful when it seems that God is not answering our prayer. How long do we keep believing that God will do the seemingly impossible?

Jesus said, "In this world you will have trouble" (John 16:33). No matter how much faith we have, the human experience includes suffering. Can we face the troubles of the world and still keep trusting God?

Hagar's declaration "You are the God who sees me" is a beautiful truth to hold on to. God's presence is with us in every difficulty and challenge we encounter. We are never alone. And we can recall that the Lord appeared to Hagar when she was most desperate. Perhaps, like Hagar, in our darkest moments God will be revealed most powerfully to us. Perhaps through suffering we become most like Christ and are best positioned to encounter God personally.

Do you know someone who is suffering? As people of faith, we have so much to offer those who are hurting! Our gracious response can be life-giving to those who feel alone in their journey. We can listen with compassion and pray; we can share our wisdom and experiences; we can inspire, encourage, and support.

4. What can we learn about how to respond to relationship tension and conflict?

All of us can relate to tension in families and breakdown in relationships. We have had to respond. Maybe we lashed out in anger and frustration like Sarah. Maybe we felt desperate and "ran away" from the conflict like Hagar. Maybe we didn't know how to respond and tried to cast the responsibility of responding to someone else, as Abraham appears to do.

This story challenges us to think deeply about how we respond and the impact of our actions—or inactions—on others. We are reminded not to mistreat others in the midst of our own trials but to bring our pain to God directly and pray for the grace to reflect Christ in our actions even when we are hurting.

For some of us, passivity is the preferred way of dealing with conflict—or *not* dealing with conflict. But this may not be what God calls us to. We can pray for courage when it is hard to stand up for what is right, especially with those closest to us.

Just like the community acknowledged Hagar's value and worth by naming a local well to commemorate her experience, we too can respond to those who are hurting by listening to and commemorating their stories. This simple act has profound effects on victims and is vital to the healing process and their ability to move forward to find meaning in suffering.

PRAYER

LORD,

You are the God who sees

In the midst of our pain, come and meet us

When we run away, bring us home

When we are desperate, speak to us

There is none unworthy of our love

There is no lowly in Your kingdom

Give us compassion to listen and hear

So Christ will be known in how we respond

Amen.

Tamar

GENESIS 38

Share one risky or bold action you've taken or would like to take one day.

BACKGROUND

Our passage begins by referencing the events of Genesis 37, when Judah and his brothers **deceived** their father, Jacob, by presenting Joseph's robe covered in blood as proof that Joseph had been attacked by wild animals and was indeed dead. In this midst of his father's grief, Judah left his family. As you read Genesis 38, you can decide if you think that Judah **continues to be detached from his family** and **avoids taking responsibility**.

Note also the motif of **clothing.** Judah's father, Jacob, gifted Joseph with a special robe. Judah used the special robe to deceive Jacob with evidence of Joseph's death. Tamar deceived Judah with clothing.

Deuteronomy 25 is a backdrop for Judah's instruction to his son to "fulfill your duty" to Tamar. In Israel, if a son dies without an heir, the law commands the next son in line to marry the widow and provide a son for his older brother so that every family line and name in Israel is preserved as a matter of identity and honor.

When Tamar is left a childless widow, she is prohibited from marrying outside of the family. The second son of Judah, Onan, is supposed to marry her and give her a child. If Onan does not want to marry Tamar, he is required to make that clear to everyone, freeing Tamar to marry outside of the family.

Deuteronomy 25 also states, "When people have a dispute, they are to take it to court and the judges will decide the case, acquitting the innocent and condemning the guilty." We are about to read whether Tamar is given an opportunity to defend herself and if any third party comes to her defense.

GENESIS

38 ¹ At that time, Judah left his brothers and went down to stay with a man of Adullam named Hirah. ² There Judah met the daughter of a Canaanite man named Shua. He married her and made love to her; ³ she became pregnant and gave birth to a son, who was named Er. ⁴ She conceived again and gave birth to a son and named him Onan. ⁵ She gave birth to still another son and named him Shelah. It was at Kezib that she gave birth to him.

⁶ Judah got a wife for Er, his firstborn, and her name was Tamar. ⁷ But Er, Judah's firstborn, was wicked in the LORD's sight; so the LORD put him to death. ⁸ Then Judah said to Onan, "Sleep with your brother's wife and fulfill your duty to her as a brother-in-law to raise up offspring for your brother." ⁹ But Onan knew that the child would not be his; so whenever he slept with his brother's wife, he spilled his semen on the ground to keep from providing offspring for his brother. ¹⁰ What he did was wicked in the LORD's sight; so the LORD put him to death also. ¹¹ Judah then said to his daughter-in-law Tamar, "Live as a widow in your father's household until my son Shelah grows up." For he thought, "He may die too, just like his brothers." So Tamar went to live in her father's household.

EXPLORE

38:1–5 Judah leaves while his father is mourning; he stays with a Canaanite (from Adullam) and marries another Canaanite; his first son is "Er" ([עֵר]), which spells "evil" backwards in Hebrew [רע]), and his second son is "Onan" (which means "wickedness"). What is your initial impression of Judah?

38:6–11 This is the only passage in Scripture where the LORD directly puts a person to death. What does this say about Judah's family line so far?

With her husband dead and Onan preventing her from conceiving a child, what options does Tamar have?

What assumption does Judah make about Tamar? (Ironically, the name Tamar means "fertility"!)

Tamar obeys her father-in-law's request. What assumption does Tamar make?

¹² After a long time Judah's wife, the daughter of Shua, died. When Judah had recovered from his grief, he went up to Timnah, to the men who were shearing his sheep, and his friend Hirah the Adullamite went with him. ¹³ When Tamar was told, "Your father-in-law is on his way to Timnah to shear his sheep," ¹⁴ she took off her widow's clothes, covered herself with a veil to disguise herself, and then sat down at the entrance to Enaim, which is on the road to Timnah. For she saw that, though Shelah had now grown up, she had not been given to him as his wife.

38:12–14 Shelah has surely grown up during this "long time." What does Tamar come to realize about Judah's plans?

Who tells Tamar about her father-in-law?

Note the role of the town reporters throughout the story. Whose side are they on?

Note the role of clothing throughout the story. Could the removal of Tamar's widow's clothes signify a change in Tamar's acceptance of her widowhood?

¹⁵ When Judah saw her, he thought she was a prostitute, for she had covered her face. ¹⁶ Not realizing that she was his daughter-in-law, he went over to her by the roadside and said, "Come now, let me sleep with you." "And what will you give me to sleep with you?" she asked. ¹⁷ "I'll send you a young goat from my flock," he said. "Will you give me something as a pledge until you send it?" she asked. ¹⁸ He said, "What pledge should I give you?" "Your seal and its cord, and the staff in your hand," she answered. So he gave them to her and slept with her, and she became pregnant by him. ¹⁹ After she left, she took off her veil and put on her widow's clothes again.

38:15–19 In what ways does the narrator emphasize that Judah is deceived?

Should Tamar's deception evoke compassion for Judah?

Is it surprising that Judah doesn't recognize Tamar's voice, even though she used to live with his family?

Does payment of a goat seem reasonable?

Why would Tamar ask for Judah's valuable items of identification—equivalent to a driver's license and ID card—as a pledge?

20 Meanwhile Judah sent the young goat by his friend the Adullamite in order to get his pledge back from the woman, but he did not find her. 21 He asked the men who lived there, "Where is the shrine prostitute who was beside the road at Enaim?" "There hasn't been any shrine prostitute here," they said. 22 So he went back to Judah and said, "I didn't find her. Besides, the men who lived there said, 'There hasn't been any shrine prostitute here.'" 23 Then Judah said, "Let her keep what she has, or we will become a laughingstock. After all, I did send her this young goat, but you didn't find her."

24 About three months later Judah was told, "Your daughter-in-law Tamar is guilty of prostitution, and as a result she is now pregnant." Judah said, "Bring her out and have her burned to death!"

38:20–23 Here we have a slightly humorous interjection where the town "reporters" confirm that Tamar was not a prostitute. Why is this ironic?

Why doesn't Judah go himself to deliver the goat?

Does Judah seem to blame his *friend* for not fulfilling the promise to Tamar?

What does Judah fear? (We will see the irony of Judah's fear as the story progresses.)

38:24 How do you respond to Judah's sentence upon Tamar?

What will Judah accomplish by eliminating Tamar—and what other lives would he be ending?

Has Tamar been given any opportunity to defend herself?

[25] As she was being brought out, she sent a message to her father-in-law. "I am pregnant by the man who owns these," she said. And she added, "See if you recognize whose seal and cord and staff these are." [26] Judah recognized them and said, "She is more righteous than I, since I wouldn't give her to my son Shelah." And he did not sleep with her again.

[27] When the time came for her to give birth, there were twin boys in her womb. [28] As she was giving birth, one of them put out his hand; so the midwife took a scarlet thread and tied it on his wrist and said, "This one came out first." [29] But when he drew back his hand, his brother came out, and she said, "So this is how you have broken out!" And he was named Perez. [30] Then his brother, who had the scarlet thread on his wrist, came out. And he was named Zerah.

38:25–26 Tamar uses the same Hebrew phrase that Judah used when deceiving his father, implying that Joseph was dead (Gen 37:32)—which could be translated "Identify, now!" in both cases. How does this phrase function as a strong condemnation of Judah?

Does verse 26 offer some redemption for Judah's wrongdoing?

38:27–30 Tamar is silent at the end of the passage. But the narrative speaks loudly for her; the blessing of two children secures her future. She is also acknowledged by later writers—Ruth 4:11–12 lists her in the line of King David, and Matthew 1:3 names Tamar in the line of Jesus Christ.

DISCUSS

1. In what ways is Tamar the victim of injustices?

2. Why is Tamar "righteous"?

3. What does this story tell us about righteousness and pursuing justice?

4. What lessons can this story teach us?

REFLECTIONS

1. In what ways is Tamar the victim of injustices?

Tamar is saddled with a husband, Er, so evil that God kills him, leaving her to be a childless widow. Biblical law practiced at that time requires Onan to "marry her and fulfill the duty of a brother-in-law to her" (Deut 25:5). But Onan does not marry Tamar, nor does he give her a child. His actions toward Tamar do not fulfill the law and seemingly are only for his personal pleasure. As such, he secretly takes advantage of Tamar, and we might say this amounts to rape. This behavior against Tamar is so wicked that the LORD kills him. Then Onan dies, leaving Tamar with even less chance for a child. Judah blames Tamar for the death of his sons and prevents her from having a child through Shelah.

Socially, she endures the pain and cultural shame of being childless, and yet she "must not marry outside the family" (Deut 25:5). Finally, Judah condemns Tamar to the cruelest punishment of death without the proper process to "take it to court and the judges will decide the case" (Deut 25:1). There is even a sense that the community is aware of what's going on (at least the town reporters), and yet there is no evidence that the community supports Tamar or defends her cause.

2. Why is Tamar "righteous"?

There are immediate textual indications of Tamar's righteousness—the townspeople who declare there is no local prostitute, Judah's declaration that vindicates her in the presence of the community, the sign of God's blessing in twins, and her position in the lineage of Christ. Also, Tamar steadfastly waits (years!) for Shelah. During this time, Tamar exhibits character, trust, and obedience, patiently waiting for Judah to fulfill his promise and the law.

More broadly, Tamar is righteous because she fights for Judah's family to preserve *his* lineage so that "the first son she bears shall carry on the name of the dead brother so that his name will not be blotted out from Israel" (Deut 25:6). Tamar does this great service for Judah and his family to ensure the future of his tribe, despite being mistreated by Judah and his sons.

Though prostitution and incest are punishable in biblical law, Tamar does right according to a more fundamental moral law to protect widows and provide security for the childless. What Tamar takes from Judah is rightfully hers—a descendant to secure her future. In this sense, her offense toward Judah is the far lesser crime, and her deception results in the fulfillment of biblical law.

Tamar's accomplishment is all the more remarkable because it is as an outsider, a Canaanite, that Tamar single-handedly preserves a tribe of Israel and establishes herself as a matriarch of Israel.

3. What does this story tell us about righteousness and pursuing justice?

Tamar lived in a culture that provided women with few options to procure personal power over their lives. Such a situation of powerlessness and victimization calls for a grace-filled understanding of righteousness. It raises questions as to how God works. (Tamar is certainly not the only Bible character to deceive and manipulate and yet be blessed by God!) Even if we are hesitant to congratulate Tamar for her scheme to bring about justice, it is clear that God has ways of measuring character and actions that might differ from our ways.

Is it possible that God calls oppressed individuals today to go so far as to *deceive* or *manipulate* to break through social limitations when the "system" fails to provide justice? For example, is it *right* if a woman lies to escape an abuser, a trafficker, or even a situation where she feels vulnerable and afraid? Is it at least *more right* than remaining under oppression and injustice?

Tamar waits for Judah to act, and when he doesn't, Tamar must find a creative solution to procure justice for herself. We may face situations where God calls us to be assertive. How should we respond when the "system" is against us? Is God calling us to assert ourselves to resolve issues of injustice?

4. What lessons can this story teach us?

Tamar demonstrates the qualities of boldness and risk-taking. When we are in a situation of mistreatment or injustice and have few options, God may call us to act boldly, take a risk, or use clever means to make things right.

Tamar teaches us about patience and the rewards of waiting. She waits a long time for Shelah to grow up; she waits by the gate for Judah; she waits to find out if she is pregnant; she waits for people to notice her protruding womb; she waits for it to be reported to Judah and then for Judah's response. She waits until the *last* possible moment to reveal the identity of the father. In the end, it is Tamar's patience and willingness to wait that causes Judah to vindicate her and ensures her survival.

This story is worth remembering when we judge others. Judah and the town reporters seemed to judge Tamar even though they didn't know some key details of what had transpired. We too can wrongly judge, and, just when we do, God may surprise us. God may bring about justice in unexpected ways—and may even use unexpected people. So, rather than assume we know how God works in all situations, we can focus our attention on supporting and helping those in trouble while trusting God with the outcome.

PRAYER

LORD,

Defend the cause of the innocent

Help those in trouble

Bring about righteousness

Establish Your kingdom on earth

Grant us

Courage to fight for what is right

Grace to do good to those who offend us

Patience as we wait for justice

Establish Your kingdom on earth

Amen.

The Midwives

EXODUS 1

Share an obstacle or challenge that God helped you overcome.

BACKGROUND

Several years after Tamar's story, a famine struck the land. Judah and his siblings discovered that Joseph (the younger brother they sold off and claimed was dead) was living in Egypt and that he had led a massive effort to fill storehouses with surplus food to sell. The whole family traveled to Joseph for refuge from the famine.

Our story begins by confirming that in the years that passed, the growing family settled permanently in Egypt and was prolific. At some point, the life-saving leadership of Joseph is forgotten. A new king arises in Egypt who feels threatened by the many Hebrew descendants.

EXODUS

1 [1] These are the names of the sons of Israel who went to Egypt with Jacob, each with his family: [2] Reuben, Simeon, Levi and Judah; [3] Issachar, Zebulun and Benjamin; [4] Dan and Naphtali; Gad and Asher. [5] The descendants of Jacob numbered seventy in all; Joseph was already in Egypt. [6] Now Joseph and all his brothers and all that generation died, [7] but the Israelites were exceedingly fruitful; they multiplied greatly, increased in numbers and became so numerous that the land was filled with them.

[8] Then a new king, to whom Joseph meant nothing, came to power in Egypt. [9] "Look," he said to his people, "the Israelites have become far too numerous for us. [10] Come, we must deal shrewdly with them or they will become even more numerous and, if war breaks out, will join our enemies, fight against us and leave the country."

EXPLORE

1:1–7 What narrative expectation is created by the opening emphasis on males?

As the story progresses, we will learn of the oppression of the Hebrews. How does the repeated emphasis on fertility indicate God's blessing on the Hebrews in the midst of their struggles?

1:8–10 What is the king's fear?

Is the king's fear legitimate or irrational?

11 So they put slave masters over them to oppress them with forced labor, and they built Pithom and Rameses as store cities for Pharaoh. 12 But the more they were oppressed, the more they multiplied and spread; so the Egyptians came to dread the Israelites 13 and worked them ruthlessly. 14 They made their lives bitter with harsh labor in brick and mortar and with all kinds of work in the fields; in all their harsh labor the Egyptians worked them ruthlessly.

1:11–14 Ironically, what does God's blessing of fertility lead to?

Does the king (Pharaoh) have a wise plan?

15 The king of Egypt said to the Hebrew midwives, whose names were Shiphrah and Puah, 16 "When you are helping the Hebrew women during childbirth on the delivery stool, if you see that the baby is a boy, kill him; but if it is a girl, let her live." 17 The midwives, however, feared God and did not do what the king of Egypt had told them to do; they let the boys live.

1:15 How is the king undermined a second time?

We can't know if the midwives are Egyptian or Hebrew with Egyptian names. Assuming the midwives are Egyptian, what do you think of their response to the king's order?

If the midwives are Hebrew, what do you think of the king's command to them?

18 Then the king of Egypt summoned the midwives and asked them, "Why have you done this? Why have you let the boys live?" 19 The midwives answered Pharaoh, "Hebrew women are not like Egyptian women; they are vigorous and give birth before the midwives arrive."

1:18–19 Is the excuse offered by the midwives believable?

The king seems to accept the midwives' reasoning. What does this indicate about him?

20 So God was kind to the midwives and the people increased and became even more numerous. 21 And because the midwives feared God, he gave them families of their own.

1:20–21 Why does God act kindly to the midwives, blessing them with families?

22 Then Pharaoh gave this order to all his people: "Every Hebrew boy that is born you must throw into the Nile, but let every girl live."

1:22 How does this final command of Pharaoh portray him?

How is this last verse a commentary on the success of the midwives?

DISCUSS

1. In what ways does God bless the Hebrews in the midst of their oppression?

2. What are some ways that the king appears foolish and weak? In contrast, how are the midwives portrayed?

3. What is required of the midwives to accomplish their mission?

4. What does the passage teach us about how God can work in a situation of powerlessness and oppression?

REFLECTIONS

1. In what ways does God bless the Hebrews in the midst of their oppression?

From the onset, we see God's blessing in the multiple references to Israel's many descendants and fertility. When the king schemes against the Hebrews, God thwarts the king's efforts by multiplying the Hebrews even more. At the pinnacle of the story, God brings literal salvation to a generation of newborn boys through the midwives. God responds to Pharaoh's second plan by again multiplying the people.

The outcomes of God's blessing continue beyond our passage as God raises up Moses from among the saved newborns, and women—perhaps inspired by the midwives—continue to work for the good of the Hebrews in defiance of the pharaoh.

In a passage where God is not often mentioned, the evidence of God's ongoing presence and blessings reminds us that God is always with us. God is always working for our good. Can we pause and reflect on God's blessings in our lives and the ways we experience God's presence in the midst of our struggles? Can we reflect on how God is bringing about salvation and life to whatever seemingly impossible situation we are facing?

2. What are some ways that the king appears foolish and weak? In contrast, how are the midwives portrayed?

The king is introduced as a weak and foolish leader. He lacks knowledge (he did not know Joseph), and he disparages his own people by declaring the Hebrews to be mightier. He is afraid of the Hebrews, and his response stirs up fear among his people. His effort to reduce the Hebrew population is ineffective—"the more they were oppressed, the more they multiplied and spread." Pharaoh wants the Hebrews to be loyal should Egypt be attacked, but his decree surely does not produce the desired outcome of loyalty. The king is unwise to expect *midwives* to kill babies, and who knows how much time passes before he realizes their defiance?! He demonstrates a lack of awareness by aiming to reduce a population by killing males (rather than future mothers!) and by believing the ridiculous idea that the birthing process and timing is determined by ethnicity. At the end of our passage, the king gives an irrational command that seemingly no one obeys.

Our heroic midwives present a stark contrast to the king. From the onset, the high birthrate of the Hebrews is witness to the skill of the midwives as instruments of God's blessing on Israel. Whereas the king commands death, the midwives bring life. While the king fears people, the midwives fear (meaning "worship" in this context) God. The king faces disloyalty, but the midwives have won the trust of the king to the point where his plan is contingent on their loyalty. Demonstrating wisdom and keen awareness of the king, the midwives see the miscalculation in his strategy and know exactly how to undermine him. The success of the midwives testifies to their cleverness, fearlessness, and strength.

If the midwives can defeat the king of Egypt, what can we accomplish for God? Maybe we think of ourselves as unexpected instruments of salvation. Maybe those around us don't have high expectations of us and lead us to undervalue ourselves. But in God's kingdom there are no social, economic, or political limitations. With confidence, we can remind ourselves that "God chose the foolish things of the world to shame the wise; God chose the weak things of the world to shame the strong" (1 Cor 1:27). Contrary to what the world would have us believe, our weaknesses actually perfectly position us to be used by God in a significant way! As 2 Corinthians 12:9 states, "My grace is sufficient for you, for my power is made perfect in weakness."

3. What is required of the midwives to accomplish their mission?

To accomplish their mission of saving lives, the midwives bravely—and discreetly—refuse to follow the king's order, requiring that they overcome fear to boldly take a great risk. Because they are restricted by limited power and authority, they must assert themselves through other methods and opt for civil disobedience to the king. By using clever means and creative thinking—or, we might say, deception—they safeguard themselves from punishment for treason and nobly bring salvation to others.

Like other women in the Bible, the midwives have a central role in fulfilling God's plan of salvation for Israel. What might be required of us to fulfill our God-given missions? What fears and self-doubts might we need to overcome to bring salvation to those in our sphere of influence? There are numerous disadvantages and limitations before us, too. Maybe these obstacles seem impossible to overcome.

The midwives had to oppose the powerful king of Egypt, but they trusted God with the outcome and accomplished something miraculous. Can we keep believing that "with God all things are possible" (Matt 19:26)? Can we focus on being faithful and responding to God's call—and trust God with the outcome?

4. What does the passage teach us about how God can work in a situation of powerlessness and oppression?

It might seem more prudent for God to send a strong political leader to confront the king's strategy. But God chooses "ordinary" women who do "ordinary" tasks—in a sense, the midwives are simply doing their jobs—for an extraordinary outcome. Surely the midwives knew they were saving some newborns, but they could not have known that 4,000 years later we would study their story and be personally inspired. Their testimony is a reminder that God calls ordinary people to accomplish great feats, and, even through ordinary acts, we can make an extraordinary impact on others.

Sometimes those who are weak and oppressed are actually not entirely powerless. The midwives were faced with an ethical dilemma—should they follow the intrinsic moral mandate to save lives or should they obey the king? They may have felt powerless, but they acted upon their conscience and, in the end, demonstrated their power to save while rendering the pharaoh powerless. We may be confronted with similar ethical dilemmas when laws of the country, expectations at work, or pressures from friends and family direct us to compromise our faith and moral convictions. When we feel oppressed, we can ask God to help us find ways to navigate the system to do what is right.

Courage: When people are in an oppressed or powerless position, it takes courage to act. The midwives risked their lives and committed treason by undermining the king's instruction. Sometimes we know the right response to a situation and we have a clear sense of God's leading, but to act requires us to have exceptional courage to refuse to compromise our integrity and to do what is right. Remember, "the one who is in you is greater than the one who is in the world" (1 John 4:4).

PRAYER

LORD,

Protect us from evildoers and oppressors

Give us courage in the midst of adversity

Be our rock and assurance in times of uncertainty

Be our light when we are surrounded by darkness

LORD,

You are the giver and sustainer of life

Make a way where we see no way

Create beauty from ashes

Bring us salvation and deliverance

Amen.

JOSHUA 2

Share a time when you experienced God's blessing in an unexpected way.

BACKGROUND

God has delivered the Hebrews from their oppression in Egypt. Now, after the Hebrews wandered in the wilderness for 40 years, God wants to establish this group of wanderers as the nation of Israel. A long speech precedes this passage where the LORD commands Joshua to lead the Israelites into the land God has given them. As the people are about to cross over the Jordan River into a new land, God's call is to be **strong** and **courageous** and to **obey**; **God's word should not leave their lips,** and they should **meditate** on it day and night.

At this pivotal moment in history, we are presented with the story of Rahab. Watch how Rahab answers God's call for strength, courage, and obedience and declares the word and acts of God.

JOSHUA

2 ¹ Then Joshua son of Nun secretly sent two spies from Shittim. "Go, look over the land," he said, "especially Jericho." So they went and entered the house of a prostitute named Rahab and stayed there.

² The king of Jericho was told, "Look, some of the Israelites have come here tonight to spy out the land." ³ So the king of Jericho sent this message to Rahab: "Bring out the men who came to you and entered your house, because they have come to spy out the whole land." ⁴ But the woman had taken the two men and hidden them. She said, "Yes, the men came to me, but I did not know where they had come from. ⁵ At dusk, when it was time to close the city gate, they left. I don't know which way they went. Go after them quickly. You may catch up with them." ⁶ (But she had taken them up to the roof and hidden them under the stalks of flax she had laid out on the roof.) ⁷ So the men set out in pursuit of the spies on the road that leads to the fords of the Jordan, and as soon as the pursuers had gone out, the gate was shut.

EXPLORE

2:1 What is Joshua's instruction?

When the men go directly to "the house of a prostitute," are they obeying Joshua's instruction?

2:2–7 The narrator does not obscure the men's visit to a prostitute; note the allusions to Hebrew euphemisms—coming, entering, knowing, and laying.

Can we assume that the "spies" were on a secret mission? If so, how secret is their mission?

At this point, why is Rahab risking her life to hide the men rather than handing them over?

8 Before the spies lay down for the night, she went up on the roof 9 and said to them, "I know that the LORD has given you this land and that a great fear of you has fallen on us, so that all who live in this country are melting in fear because of you. 10 We have heard how the LORD dried up the water of the Red Sea for you when you came out of Egypt, and what you did to Sihon and Og, the two kings of the Amorites east of the Jordan, whom you completely destroyed. 11 When we heard of it, our hearts melted in fear and everyone's courage failed because of you, for the LORD your God is God in heaven above and on the earth below.

12 "Now then, please swear to me by the LORD that you will show kindness to my family, because I have shown kindness to you. Give me a sure sign 13 that you will spare the lives of my father and mother, my brothers and sisters, and all who belong to them—and that you will save us from death." 14 "Our lives for your lives!" the men assured her. "If you don't tell what we are doing, we will treat you kindly and faithfully when the LORD gives us the land." 15 So she let them down by a rope through the window, for the house she lived in was part of the city wall. 16 She said to them, "Go to the hills so the pursuers will not find you. Hide yourselves there three days until they return, and then go on your way."

2:8–11 In what sense does Rahab's speech fulfill the men's objective to survey the land?

Where has Rahab heard about the LORD and the miraculous acts of God on behalf of Israel?

What does Rahab's strong theological statement in verse 11 indicate about her faith?

2:12–16 Rahab is sure that the Israelites will conquer her town, Jericho. What does this say about her belief in the God of Israel?

The men (now!) declare faith in the LORD— what has prompted their confidence?

[22] When they left, they went into the hills and stayed there three days, until the pursuers had searched all along the road and returned without finding them. [23] Then the two men started back. They went down out of the hills, forded the river and came to Joshua son of Nun and told him everything that had happened to them. [24] They said to Joshua, "The LORD has surely given the whole land into our hands; all the people are melting in fear because of us."

2:22–24 Do the men obey Rahab's instructions?

Rahab predicts the men will return home safely, and they do. What expectation does this create for Rahab's prophecy of Israel's victory over Jericho?

What is the source of the men's report?

The men's mission is complete—but have they done any spying?

6 [24] Then they burned the whole city and everything in it, but they put the silver and gold and the articles of bronze and iron into the treasury of the LORD's house. [25] But Joshua spared Rahab the prostitute, with her family and all who belonged to her, because she hid the men Joshua had sent as spies to Jericho—and she lives among the Israelites to this day.

6:24–25 In the end, who all are saved by Rahab's actions?

The genealogy in Matthew 1 records Rahab as the mother of Boaz, an ancestor of King David, and a distant ancestor of Jesus. If this is indeed the same Rahab, what impact does she have on Israel's history?

DISCUSS

1. How is Rahab's identification as a prostitute significant?

2. What do we learn about God in this passage—and who tells us?

3. Is Rahab justified in lying to save the lives of the spies of Israel?

4. How is Rahab's faithful obedience to God an example for Israel and us?

REFLECTIONS

1. How is Rahab's identification as a prostitute significant?

As a prostitute, Rahab may seem an unlikely instrument of God's salvation. Yet her situation plays a key role in her ministry. Likely, her customers reveal the fear that grips her city—information Rahab passes on that gives Joshua a strategic military advantage. These customers report all that God did for Israel, which inspires Rahab's belief in the God of Israel and confidence in Israel's forthcoming victory. Her theological declaration forms the core of the men's report to Joshua. When the men come to Rahab, she has means to provide lodging for them and then hide them from the king. Her location on the city wall enables her to know the routines of the king's men and helps the spies escape.

Rahab's occupation as a prostitute is significant in the broader biblical narrative. Traditionally, Rahab is considered the mother of Boaz, who also acts for the redemption of others in the story of Naomi and Ruth. This places Rahab in the line of Jesus. This doesn't mean that her occupation is condoned, but it reveals that the God Rahab feared chose to come to earth through her lineage. Further, the New Testament applauds Rahab's "faith" (Heb 11:31) and commends her as "righteous" (Jas 2:25).

It is easy to underestimate people who seem to have little significance. Not so in God's kingdom. The LORD uses whatever skills and resources we have for God's glory. How encouraging! It also reminds us to "accept one another, then, just as Christ accepted [us]" (Rom 15:7).

2. What do we learn about God in this passage—and who tells us?

Rahab's speech to the men is profound. The men have said nothing about God, yet Rahab delivers a persuasive sermon. She begins by prophesying that the LORD will give Israel the land. With confidence, she presents what God is about to do as fact—and indeed, her words are fulfilled, confirming that her prediction was true. This is remarkable because, unlike the spies, Rahab has only *heard* of who God is and what God has done; she has not personally witnessed God's great deeds (yet!).

Next, Rahab accurately recounts the recent mighty acts of God for Israel. Her sermon ends with a theological declaration that the LORD God "is God in heaven above and on earth below." By this statement, Rahab affirms that the God of Israel is mightier than all other local gods, that the God of Israel is supreme. Her words recall Deuteronomy 4, where Moses admonishes Israel: "Acknowledge and take to heart this day that the LORD is God in heaven above and on the earth below" (39).

Rahab is surely an unlikely source of theological teaching, but this seems to be exactly how God often works!

3. Is Rahab justified in lying to save the lives of the spies of Israel?

Rahab must make a perilous decision: reveal the whereabouts of the men, and they will be killed, or lie, and the men might escape. It is certainly in Rahab's best interest to tell the truth and save herself. But Rahab chooses the self-sacrificial option to save the men's lives. She chooses to believe and obey the God of Israel and works to save the lives of the people of Israel, even though her actions lead to the deaths of her own people. Importantly, Rahab is not an Israelite and as such does not live under the laws given to Israel.

This story challenges an unequivocal view of ethics. We can agree that lying is wrong and we should avoid it. But we should also acknowledge that to save lives is to do God's work on earth. Rahab sought to save lives through deception—and God rewarded her actions. As with real-life situations, we are challenged to work out what it means to follow God in Rahab's circumstances. But we can look to the conclusion of the story for a way forward—God blesses Rahab by saving her family and establishing her within Israel. When we wrestle with a choice that presents a moral dilemma, we can pray for discernment to know which path will yield life and salvation for others.

4. How is Rahab's faithful obedience to God an example for Israel and us?

The LORD admonishes Joshua to be strong, courageous, and obedient while speaking and meditating on God's word (Josh 1). Rahab exemplifies these traits and speaks of God in the story that follows. She courageously risks her life for the people of Israel to the peril of her own people. Rahab believes in the God of Israel and fulfills Israel's calling to declare the acts of God to others. In these ways, she leads the way forward, in faithful obedience to God, for Israel to follow.

By saving the lives of the men—even by deception—Rahab demonstrates the biblical principle "To do what is right and just is more acceptable to the LORD than sacrifice" (Prov 21:3). We are reminded, "The LORD does not look at the things people look at. People look at the outward appearance, but the LORD looks at the heart" (1 Sam 16:7).

If Rahab, a non-Israelite and a prostitute, can lead in faithfulness, surely we can follow her example. In what areas is God calling us to be strong and courageous? Can we, like Rahab, offer to God whatever skills and resources we have to build God's kingdom here on earth?

PRAYER

Lord,

You have done incredible deeds for Your people
We ask You to act again for Your people in our time

You are the God who fights our battles
We ask You for victory

We reflect on who You are
And our hearts are filled with hope

You have already done many great things for us
Therefore, we tell of Your deeds

We declare that You are God above and rule over the heavens
And You are God below, with us, and rule over earth

Amen.

THE BOOK OF RUTH

Share about someone you know who shows self-sacrificial love.

BACKGROUND

This story occurs during the **time of the judges**, which was after Joshua's leadership during the days of Rahab and before the monarchy was established in Israel. There was no centralized leadership; numerous judges led Israel through various crises, even though they generally lacked personal character. The last verse of the book of Judges provides a negative perspective of this time period: "In those days Israel had no king; everyone did as they saw fit" (21:25).

In this context of immorality, Naomi's faith is exemplary.

RUTH

1 ¹ In the days when the judges ruled, there was a famine in the land. So a man from Bethlehem in Judah, together with his wife and two sons, went to live for a while in the country of Moab. ² The man's name was Elimelek, his wife's name was Naomi, and the names of his two sons were Mahlon and Kilion ... ³ Now Elimelek, Naomi's husband, died, and she was left with her two sons. ⁴ They married Moabite women, one named Orpah and the other Ruth. After they had lived there about ten years, ⁵ both Mahlon and Kilion also died, and Naomi was left without her two sons and her husband.

⁶ When Naomi heard in Moab that the LORD had come to the aid of his people by providing food for them, she and her daughters-in-law prepared to return home from there. ⁷ With her two daughters-in-law she left the place where she had been living and set out on the road that would take them back to the land of Judah. ⁸ Then Naomi said to her two daughters-in-law, "Go back, each of you, to your mother's home. May the LORD show you kindness, as you have shown kindness to your dead husbands and to me. ⁹ May the LORD grant that each of you will find rest in the home of another husband."

EXPLORE

1:1–5 In this opening scene, what sorrow and loss befall Naomi?

1:6–9 How does Naomi exemplify leadership to her daughters-in-law?

How does Naomi exemplify selflessness?

14 Orpah kissed her mother-in-law goodbye, but Ruth clung to her. 15 "Look," said Naomi, "your sister-in-law is going back to her people and her gods. Go back with her." 16 But Ruth replied, "Don't urge me to leave you or to turn back from you. Where you go I will go, and where you stay I will stay. Your people will be my people and your God my God. 17 Where you die I will die, and there I will be buried. May the LORD deal with me, be it ever so severely, if even death separates you and me."

1:14–17 What does Ruth's fierce loyalty suggest about Naomi's character and leadership?

How has Ruth developed such a strong commitment to the God of Israel while living in a nation that does not worship the God of Israel?

19 When [the two women] arrived in Bethlehem, the whole town was stirred because of them, and the women exclaimed, "Can this be Naomi?" 20 "Don't call me Naomi," she told them. "Call me Mara, because the Almighty has made my life very bitter. 21 I went away full, but the LORD has brought me back empty. Why call me Naomi? The LORD has afflicted me; the Almighty has brought misfortune upon me."

1:19–21 Naomi means "pleasant" and Mara means "bitter." What does Naomi's desire to be called Mara reveal about how she is feeling?

Has Naomi maintained faith amid her pain and suffering?

The townswomen offer no reply to Naomi. Why might they be silent?

[Ruth goes to "work" in a field to collect harvest leftovers for her and Naomi. It turns out the field belongs to a relative of Naomi, and this man, Boaz, the son of Rahab according to the traditional interpretation of Matthew 1, notices Ruth. He is very kind and generous toward her.] **2** [19] Her mother-in-law asked her, "Where did you glean today? Where did you work? Blessed be the man who took notice of you!" Then Ruth told her mother-in-law about the one at whose place she had been working ... [20] "The LORD bless him!" Naomi said to her daughter-in-law. "He has not stopped showing his kindness to the living and the dead." She added, "That man is our close relative; he is one of our guardian-redeemers."

2:19–20 When a widow is childless, biblical law requires the closest male relative to provide for her as a guardian. How does Naomi's speech infuse hope into the narrative?

3 ¹ One day Ruth's mother-in-law Naomi said to her, "My daughter, I must find a home for you, where you will be well provided for. ² Now Boaz, with whose women you have worked, is a relative of ours. Tonight he will be winnowing barley on the threshing floor. ³ Wash, put on perfume, and get dressed in your best clothes. Then go down to the threshing floor, but don't let him know you are there until he has finished eating and drinking. ⁴ When he lies down, note the place where he is lying. Then go and uncover his feet and lie down. He will tell you what to do."

[Ruth follows Naomi's plan, and Boaz offers to marry Ruth if another guardian-redeemer who is legally first in line does not agree to accept his obligation to the women.]

3:1−4 These instructions, replete with Hebrew euphemisms, form rather scandalous advice. Does this suggest a further change in Naomi's perspective on life, that she is moving forward despite her sorrow?

[16] When Ruth came to her mother-in-law, Naomi asked, "How did it go, my daughter?" Then she told her everything Boaz had done for her [17] and added, "He gave me these six measures of barley, saying, 'Don't go back to your mother-in-law empty-handed.'" [18] Then Naomi said, "Wait, my daughter, until you find out what happens. For the man will not rest until the matter is settled today."

[The kinsman redeemer who is the closest family member relinquishes his responsibility to Boaz.]

4 [9] Then Boaz announced to the elders and all the people, "Today you are witnesses that I have bought from Naomi all the property of Elimelek, Kilion and Mahlon. [10] I have also acquired Ruth the Moabite, Mahlon's widow, as my wife, in order to maintain the name of the dead with his property, so that his name will not disappear from among his family or from his hometown. Today you are witnesses!"

3:16–18 How does Naomi demonstrate discernment and wisdom in her instruction for Ruth to wait?

4:9–10 How does Naomi's care for Ruth result in blessing for Naomi?

[11] Then the elders and all the people at the gate said, "We are witnesses. May the LORD make the woman who is coming into your home like Rachel and Leah, who together built up the family of Israel. May you have standing in Ephrathah and be famous in Bethlehem. [12] Through the offspring the LORD gives you by this young woman, may your family be like that of Perez, whom Tamar bore to Judah." [13] So Boaz took Ruth and she became his wife. When he made love to her, the LORD enabled her to conceive, and she gave birth to a son.

4:11–13 Although God cannot remove the pain of Naomi's losses, to what extent has God redeemed her from the afflictions she endured?

[14] The women said to Naomi: "Praise be to the LORD, who this day has not left you without a guardian-redeemer. May he become famous throughout Israel! [15] He will renew your life and sustain you in your old age. For your daughter-in-law, who loves you and who is better to you than seven sons, has given him birth."

4:14–15 How does this speech bring value and worth to Naomi?

How does the women's response here compare to their earlier silence?

¹⁶ Then Naomi took the child in her arms and cared for him. ¹⁷ The women living there said, "Naomi has a son!" And they named him Obed.

4:16–17 What is noteworthy about the women using the name Naomi?

The name Obed is rooted in "service/work" or "servant." Why do the women choose this name?

How has Naomi's life gained meaning and purpose after her suffering?

¹⁸ This, then, is the family line of Perez: …
²¹… Boaz the father of Obed,
²² Obed the father of Jesse,
and Jesse the father of David.

4:18–22 The book of Ruth ends with a genealogy. What legacy does Naomi provide for her descendants?

Can you think of any ways that David's life and character reflect Naomi's legacy?

DISCUSS

1. What are Naomi's struggles, and how does she respond?

2. What does Naomi teach us about leading our families?

3. What can we learn about community from this story?

4. In what ways does Naomi reflect a life well-lived that we can emulate?

REFLECTIONS

1. What are Naomi's struggles, and how does she respond?

Sorrow is first indicated by the news that Naomi had to leave her hometown. A natural disaster—famine—leads to Naomi's displacement. She is cut off from her community and support system and must begin a new life in a country very different from her own—with two boys. Does she know the language? Does she meet anyone who shares her culture and religion?

Her isolation is heightened by the loss of her husband and sons. Naomi is left with two daughters-in-law to care for, yet it appears she has few resources. Returning "home" presents a second displacement for Naomi after she has settled in Moab. Surely she returns to her hometown in some senses a stranger after being absent so long.

Naomi's bitterness is reflected in her chosen name, Mara, which reflects the disorder in her life. And despite her faith, she presents the LORD as against her. Her bitterness is from the LORD, who has afflicted her and brought her misfortune.

To maintain that God has allowed the crisis to occur—or even that God brought it about—is to trust that God can also bring restoration. As long as God is in control and good, the world has order and meaning. In a time of crisis, the belief that God is still in control is essential for the person of faith. So Naomi does not forsake God; she perseveres in faith.

2. What does Naomi teach us about leading our families?

The passage opens with events happening *to* Naomi. But after multiple tragedies strike, Naomi is no longer willing to remain a passive character. Naomi learns of what the LORD is doing in her homeland. She acts on this knowledge to bring her daughters-in-law to a place of God's provision and aid. In this, Naomi demonstrates leadership in a time of adversity.

As she is taking the journey back to her home, she takes account of the circumstances of her daughters-in-law. Surely their presence is a comfort to Naomi and a last connection to her sons. Yet, she is willing to let them go for their own sakes so they can create a future for themselves in their own land, saving them from the displacement she herself experienced. She resolves that her loss will not determine the future of her daughters-in-law. By putting her daughters-in-law first, Naomi reveals great selflessness amid her sorrow.

The loyalty of Ruth suggests that Naomi is an exemplary mother. We can surmise that Ruth stays with Naomi because she is a loving, kind, and good person. She provides support and inner strength for Ruth despite her lack of worldly wealth. As the story progresses, Naomi's wisdom and discernment lead Ruth to secure her future with Boaz. Naomi's commitment to her family is revealed again in her immediate care for her grandchild.

As matriarch of the family, Naomi's influence is perceived in the loyalty, love, and selflessness featured throughout the story. What examples do we provide for our families—immediate and extended? Do we offer support in the midst of our own struggles? Are we examples to our families and loved ones of how to maintain faith during tragedy and difficulty? Do we demonstrate loyalty even when we are wronged? Do we point our family to Christ?

3. What can we learn about community from this story?

The community of women rejoice when Naomi returns, but they react to her tale of woe with silence. Their lack of response illustrates the challenge of bringing appropriate words and acts of comfort to those who have suffered trauma or loss. When we have the opportunity to provide comfort to others, how should we respond?

Our first response can be to listen. By doing so, we offer the consolation of the ministry of our presence. In the moments we are together—and through prayer—we "mourn with those who mourn" (Rom 12:15). Our simple presence creates an opportunity for those who are suffering to find healing, to share the heaviness of their burdens. Community assures those who suffer that they are not alone. It gives us the opportunity to share and be Christ to others. Because the Spirit of Christ indwells us, we can experience the presence of God through fellow-believers. How needed is this ministry of presence in our world of increasing isolation!

When we must say something, we can talk about God's character, God's mercy, and God's care. We can offer hope in God's compassionate, long-suffering, gracious nature. Are we called upon to pray in the most impossible, painful moments? Let us begin by declaring the compassionate nature of God and then asking for God's mercy to restore and heal the situation.

The women in Naomi's community offer a much different response to the joyful news of her grandchild. Their praise and blessing remind us of the importance of community to rejoice and celebrate together and to declare God's goodness and blessings!

4. In what ways does Naomi reflect a life well-lived that we can emulate?

Naomi's close bond with Ruth is one of the most beautiful relationships in the Bible. Despite her sorrow and loss, Naomi loves and cares for this "daughter" deeply. How tender too that Ruth brings Naomi hope through loyalty and companionship—and later provides Naomi with a second family. Who has God placed in your life to love and care for? Are you called to bring hope and life to someone in your sphere?

Throughout the story, we find Naomi patiently waiting, and even instructing Ruth to wait for Boaz. Though God doesn't erase Naomi's loss, in time, God rebuilds her life. When we walk through seasons of sorrow and bitterness, are we willing to patiently wait for God? Can we maintain hope for God to one day restore our joy and happiness?

Many of us can look back and see how God turned a bad situation for good or restored our broken hearts over time. Our stories are worth sharing, even if only to encourage each other about God's faithfulness!

PRAYER

Lord,

You say to us,

"Come to Me, all you who are weary and burdened,
and I will give you rest.
Take My yoke upon you and learn from Me,
for I am gentle and humble in heart,
and you will find rest for your souls."

Lord,

Grant us the joy of loving relationships
Bless us with true companionship

Heal the hearts that have been broken
Hold close those who are alone, those who suffer loss

Restore families that are hurting
Return home those far away

Help us lead our families to You
To love like Christ in all that we do

Amen.

(Scripture taken from Matthew 11:28–29)

Hannah

1 SAMUEL 1-2

Share about a time when you had to wait patiently for God to answer your prayer.

BACKGROUND

Hannah lives during the **time of the judges**, as Naomi did. Hannah's faithfulness stands in contrast to the immorality that is characteristic of this period. While many in Israel are far from God, Hannah exhibits a personal relationship with God that changes the course of Israel's history.

1 SAMUEL

1 ¹ There was a certain man from Ramathaim, a Zuphite from the hill country of Ephraim, whose name was Elkanah son of Jeroham, the son of Elihu, the son of Tohu, the son of Zuph, an Ephraimite. ² He had two wives; one was called Hannah and the other Peninnah. Peninnah had children, but Hannah had none. ³ Year after year this man went up from his town to worship and sacrifice to the LORD Almighty at Shiloh, where Hophni and Phinehas, the two sons of Eli, were priests of the LORD. ⁴ Whenever the day came for Elkanah to sacrifice, he would give portions of the meat to his wife Peninnah and to all her sons and daughters. ⁵ But to Hannah he gave a double portion because he loved her, and the LORD had closed her womb.

EXPLORE

1:1–5 What are the signs of faithfulness in Hannah's family?

What are the signs of trouble in Hannah's family?

Recall how Sarah, Hagar, and Tamar responded to the crisis surrounding infertility and childlessness. Watch for how Hannah's response differs.

6 Because the LORD had closed Hannah's womb, her rival kept provoking her in order to irritate her. 7 This went on year after year. Whenever Hannah went up to the house of the LORD, her rival provoked her till she wept and would not eat. 8 Her husband Elkanah would say to her, "Hannah, why are you weeping? Why don't you eat? Why are you downhearted? Don't I mean more to you than ten sons?"

9 Once when they had finished eating and drinking in Shiloh, Hannah stood up. Now Eli the priest was sitting on his chair by the doorpost of the LORD's house. 10 In her deep anguish Hannah prayed to the LORD, weeping bitterly. 11 And she made a vow, saying, "LORD Almighty, if you will only look on your servant's misery and remember me, and not forget your servant but give her a son, then I will give him to the LORD for all the days of his life, and no razor will ever be used on his head."

1:6–8 How do you think Hannah felt knowing that God had closed her womb and then being subjected to Peninnah's ongoing taunting?

Do you expect someone to come to Hannah's defense against Peninnah?

Is Elkanah's response helpful?

What does Hannah's lack of response to Elkanah indicate?

1:9–11 Hannah stands—could this reflect a change in her perspective?

"Deep anguish" could be translated as "depression."

What does Hannah's prayer reveal about her relationship with God?

[12] As she kept on praying to the LORD, Eli observed her mouth. [13] Hannah was praying in her heart, and her lips were moving but her voice was not heard. Eli thought she was drunk [14] and said to her, "How long are you going to stay drunk? Put away your wine."

1:12–14 What would you normally expect from a priest in this heart-wrenching moment?

Is it possible that Eli's chiding deepens Hannah's sense of aloneness?

[15] "Not so, my lord," Hannah replied, "I am a woman who is deeply troubled. I have not been drinking wine or beer; I was pouring out my soul to the LORD. [16] Do not take your servant for a wicked woman; I have been praying here out of my great anguish and grief." [17] Eli answered, "Go in peace, and may the God of Israel grant you what you have asked of him." [18] She said, "May your servant find favor in your eyes." Then she went her way and ate something, and her face was no longer downcast.

1:15–18 How does Hannah receive Eli's blessing?

What does Hannah's response to Eli indicate about her character?

Does verse 18 indicate a change within Hannah?

[19] Early the next morning they arose and worshiped before the LORD and then went back to their home at Ramah. Elkanah made love to his wife Hannah, and the LORD remembered her. [20] So in the course of time Hannah became pregnant and gave birth to a son. She named him Samuel, saying, "Because I asked the LORD for him."

1:19–20 The name Samuel means "heard by God" or "name of God." How does Hannah's choice of name for her son reflect her perspective of all that has happened?

21 When her husband Elkanah went up with all his family to offer the annual sacrifice to the LORD and to fulfill his vow, 22 Hannah did not go. She said to her husband, "After the boy is weaned, I will take him and present him before the LORD, and he will live there always." 23 "Do what seems best to you," her husband Elkanah told her. "Stay here until you have weaned him; only may the LORD make good his word."

So the woman stayed at home and nursed her son until she had weaned him. 24 After he was weaned, she took the boy with her, young as he was, along with a three-year-old bull, an ephah of flour and a skin of wine, and brought him to the house of the LORD at Shiloh. 25 When the bull had been sacrificed, they brought the boy to Eli, 26 and she said to him, "Pardon me, my lord. As surely as you live, I am the woman who stood here beside you praying to the LORD. 27 I prayed for this child, and the LORD has granted me what I asked of him. 28 So now I give him to the LORD. For his whole life he will be given over to the LORD." And he worshiped the LORD there … 2 19 Each year his mother made him a little robe and took it to him when she went up with her husband to offer the annual sacrifice.

1:21–23 Now Hannah must fulfill her vow to give the child back to God to minister before the LORD. Why does Hannah resist the (fateful!) trip to Shiloh?

Why would Elkanah admonish Hannah to fulfill her vow?

1:23–28, 2:19 Can you discern narrative details that indicate Hannah's tender love for her child?

Despite the priest Eli's earlier rebuke, how does Hannah respond to Eli here?

²⁰ Eli would bless Elkanah and his wife, saying, "May the LORD give you children by this woman to take the place of the one she prayed for and gave to the LORD." Then they would go home. ²¹ And the LORD was gracious to Hannah; she gave birth to three sons and two daughters. Meanwhile, the boy Samuel grew up in the presence of the LORD.

2:20–21 To what extent does the end of this narrative provide closure and resolution to Hannah's desire for a child?

The name Hannah means "grace" and "favor." In what ways are grace and favor central themes in this story?

DISCUSS

1. What struggles does Hannah face?

2. What can we learn from how Hannah responds to her challenges?

3. How does Hannah demonstrate spiritual leadership and provide a model for future leaders?

4. How does Hannah establish a foundation for her child's life and ministry through her example?

REFLECTIONS

1. What struggles does Hannah face?

Hannah endures the sorrow of infertility and childlessness. In a culture where progeny is essential for a woman's survival and status, we can assume that Hannah experiences social humiliation associated with her infertility. To make matters worse, she lives with a woman and children who are daily reminders of what she lacks. Hannah's husband loves her but seems unaware of how to comfort her. Amplifying her isolation, Eli the priest rebukes her in a very sacred moment of anguish before the LORD. Most painful of all must surely be Hannah's belief that the LORD has caused her agony.

2. What can we learn from how Hannah responds to her challenges?

From the onset, Hannah puts God at the center of her life. She believes that God is in control of her life—it is God who closed her womb, and God has the power to heal her. Infertility creates deep heartache for Hannah, and she brings her pain to the LORD in prayer. Even in her suffering, Hannah is gracious—showing no vindictiveness to Peninnah and responding to Eli's rebuke with respect.

The humility in Hannah's prayer to God is profoundly moving. Though the LORD has caused her pain, she surrenders to God's will and vows to give back to God her greatest desire. Her great faith in God's ability to answer her prayer is demonstrated when she leaves Eli—her face is no longer depressed, even before she has any sign that God will give her a child.

There is perhaps a second heartache in this story. It is the moment Hannah must leave her son with Eli. Yet, Hannah fulfills her promise to God in faithful obedience.

We all endure times of anguish. Do we let our heartache drive us to God? Do we bring our sorrow to God in prayer? Do we humbly accept that God is in control even when we are suffering? Can we find a way to trust God with the outcome?

Anger and doubt are natural responses; unwavering faith is a much harder response. How can we maintain our faith and commitment to God in seasons of great pain and difficulty?

3. How does Hannah demonstrate spiritual leadership and provide a model for future leaders?

The narrator has intentionally placed the story of Hannah at the beginning of the history books. Hannah honors God through faithful sacrifice, fulfills her vow to God, demonstrates a personal relationship with God, believes God is all powerful, triumphs over her enemy, and witnesses the miraculous work of God. This is exactly what the people of Israel need to do. Israel must cast aside its idolatry and fulfill its vows of obedience to God. They must take personal responsibility to worship, believe, obey, and trust God. Then they will be victorious over their enemies and enjoy God's blessing and protection on a national scale. Sadly, Israel ultimately fails to heed Hannah's example, and so this narrative serves in part as an exposé of why the people end up in exile.

The life of Hannah teaches us about leadership during hard times. Hannah is misunderstood, even by her loving husband, and feels isolated. Like Jeremiah and others, Hannah suffers anguish and depression but does not lose faith in God.

We can expect to encounter rejection and judgment as leaders, and we will experience loneliness. Hannah's response to go to the house of God and pray is exemplary. Her prayer is earnest and honest; she leaves God's presence with expectation. We too can pray with earnestness and honesty and then trust that God has heard our prayer and will answer. God's answer may not be exactly as we want or in the timing we desire, but we can trust that God is working for our good and cares about our every need.

4. How does Hannah establish a foundation for her child's life and ministry through her example?

Hannah's miraculous child, Samuel, becomes a great leader in Israel. He leads Israel from being a collection of tribes to a monarchy with a centralized government. Samuel is regarded as a righteous leader, and his ministry to Israel is marked by a personal relationship with God, prayer, prophetic speech, close ties (and friction) with the priesthood, and faithful service amid adversity. Does this sound familiar? There is no doubt that Samuel's character and leadership reflect his mother's example.

Just as Samuel's life is a legacy of the influence of a godly mother, we too may have a great impact on the people around us. We can lead our family in spiritual practices. We can share our faith with our friends and neighbors. We can serve others in ways that embody the message of Christ.

We all have opportunities to make an impact—in our workplaces, churches, neighborhoods, and homes. God has placed us in community, and one way we can show gratitude for all God has done for us is to inspire faith in the people in our lives and lead them to Christ. Like Hannah, we may never know the impact of our legacy on others!

PRAYER

LORD,

We come to you in prayer
We come to you in humility
We come trusting Your word

We bring our anguish
We bring our aloneness
We bring our heartache

We ask for Your healing
We ask for Your restoration
We ask to have greater faith

We offer to You the words of Hannah:

"The LORD is a God who knows ...
There is no one besides You ...
My heart rejoices in the LORD ...
I delight in Your deliverance"

Amen.

(Scripture taken from 1 Samuel 2.)

THE BOOK OF ESTHER

Who are the people that you influence and lead?

BACKGROUND

Esther's story takes place toward the end of Old Testament history. The time of the judges has given way to the monarchy. Soon after the monarchy is established, the unified kingdom of Israel splits into the two nations of Israel and Judah. Several hundred years later, Israel is conquered by the kingdom of Assyria. Eventually, Judah is conquered by the kingdom of Babylon. These nations took the people of Israel and Judah into exile. In time, the Persian kingdom arose and defeated Babylon.

In their new lands, the exiles from Israel and Judah are called Jews. Esther and her uncle, Mordecai, are descendants of these exiles, who settled in the foreign land and created Jewish communities.

We see in the book of Esther that some powerful people in Persia hate the Jews. Even in exile, after being taken hostage, the people of God still face enemies.

ESTHER

1 [1] This is what happened during the time of Xerxes ... [4] For a full 180 days he displayed the vast wealth of his kingdom and the splendor and glory of his majesty. [5] ... the king gave a banquet, lasting seven days, in the enclosed garden of the king's palace ... [6] The garden had hangings of white and blue linen, fastened with cords of white linen and purple material to silver rings on marble pillars. There were couches of gold and silver on a mosaic pavement of porphyry, marble, mother-of-pearl and other costly stones. [7] Wine was served in goblets of gold ...

[The king commands the queen to display her beauty before the guests, but Queen Vashti refuses. The queen is banished, and a search begins for a new queen.]

EXPLORE

1:1–7 Note the opulence, wealth, and power of the king and the expanse of Persia. How does this opening description of the vastness of Persia contrast with the life of a young Jewish girl living as an exile?

When we think about Persia's great power and the political tension created by the queen's response, how does it compare to our social-political situation today?

2 **5** Now there was in the citadel of Susa a Jew … named Mordecai … **6** who had been carried into exile from Jerusalem … **7** Mordecai had a cousin … Esther, [who] had a lovely figure and was beautiful. Mordecai had taken her as his own daughter when her father and mother died. **8** When the king's order and edict had been proclaimed … Esther also was taken to the king's palace and entrusted to Hegai, who had charge of the harem. **9** She pleased him and won his favor.

2:5–9 From these few lines, what do we learn about Esther's character and identity at the time she is taken to the king's palace?

15 When the turn came for Esther … to go to the king, she asked for nothing other than what Hegai … suggested. And Esther won the favor of everyone who saw her … **17** Now the king was attracted to Esther more than to any of the other women, and she won his favor and approval more than any of the other virgins. So he set a royal crown on her head and made her queen.

2:15–17 Even though Esther is living in exile and is taken hostage to a very powerful king, how is God at work in her life and blessing her?

[20] But Esther had kept secret her family background and nationality just as Mordecai had told her to do, for she continued to follow Mordecai's instructions as she had done when he was bringing her up. [21] During the time Mordecai was sitting at the king's gate, Bigthana and Teresh, two of the king's officers who guarded the doorway, became angry and conspired to assassinate King Xerxes. [22] But Mordecai found out about the plot and told Queen Esther, who in turn reported it to the king, giving credit to Mordecai.

[Later, a top noble, Haman, was honored by royal officials, but Mordecai would not bow to Haman. Infuriated, Haman devised to kill Mordecai—and all the Jews. Mordecai relayed this to Esther, who was greatly distressed at the news.]

2:20–22 How does Esther exhibit wisdom?

What character traits does Esther display in saving the life of a king who took her hostage to the palace?

Why does Haman develop such hatred toward the Jews?

4 [8] [Mordecai instructed Esther] to go into the king's presence to beg for mercy and plead with him for her people … [13] … "Do not think that because you are in the king's house you alone of all the Jews will escape. [14] For if you remain silent at this time, relief and deliverance for the Jews will arise from another place, but you and your father's family will perish. And who knows but that you have come to your royal position for such a time as this?" [15] Then Esther sent this reply to Mordecai: [16] "Go, gather together all the Jews who are in Susa, and fast for me. Do not eat or drink for three days, night or day. I and my attendants will fast as you do. When this is done, I will go to the king, even though it is against the law. And if I perish, I perish."

4:8–16 Mordecai assumes that Esther will also be killed—is there any evidence that he is correct?

Esther responds to Mordecai's compelling call to act. In what ways does Esther's response provide leadership to her people?

5 ¹ On the third day Esther put on her royal robes and stood in the inner court of the palace, in front of the king's hall ... ² When he saw Queen Esther standing in the court, he was pleased with her and held out to her the gold scepter that was in his hand. So Esther approached and touched the tip of the scepter. ³ Then the king asked, "What is it, Queen Esther? What is your request? Even up to half the kingdom, it will be given you." ⁴ "If it pleases the king," replied Esther, "let the king, together with Haman, come today to a banquet I have prepared for him." ⁵ ... So the king and Haman went to the banquet Esther had prepared. ⁶ As they were drinking wine, the king again asked Esther, "Now what is your petition? ..." ⁷ Esther replied, "My petition and my request is this: ⁸ If the king regards me with favor and if it pleases the king to grant my petition and fulfill my request, let the king and Haman come tomorrow to the banquet I will prepare for them. Then I will answer the king's question."

[That night, the king recalls when a plot against his life was foiled by Mordecai, which we read about earlier. The next day, he commissions Haman to parade Mordecai through the city to honor him.]

5:1–8 What character traits does Esther display as she feasts with her enemy Haman?

And what character traits does Esther display when she delays her request of the king for another day?

What is ironic about Haman publicly honoring Mordecai?

How does this scene provide hope for Esther and testify to what God is able to do for her and the Jews?

7 ¹ So the king and Haman went to Queen Esther's banquet, ² and as they were drinking wine on the second day, the king again asked, "Queen Esther, what is your petition? It will be given you. What is your request? Even up to half the kingdom, it will be granted." ³ Then Queen Esther answered, "If I have found favor with you, Your Majesty, and if it pleases you, grant me my life—this is my petition. And spare my people—this is my request. ⁴ For I and my people have been sold to be destroyed, killed and annihilated. If we had merely been sold as male and female slaves, I would have kept quiet, because no such distress would justify disturbing the king."

7:1–4 Before we even know the king's response and the outcome of the story, how does this passage present Esther as a heroine to her people?

[The king hangs Haman on the pole that Haman had intended for Mordecai. Then, the king gives Queen Esther the estate of Haman and promotes Mordecai to replace Haman.]

8 ³ Esther again pleaded with the king, falling at his feet and weeping. She begged him to put an end to the evil plan of Haman the Agagite, which he had devised against the Jews. ⁴ Then the king extended the gold scepter to Esther and she arose and stood before him. ⁵ "If it pleases the king," she said, "and if he regards me with favor and thinks it the right thing to do, and if he is pleased with me, let an order be written overruling the dispatches that Haman son of Hammedatha, the Agagite, devised and wrote to destroy the Jews in all the king's provinces. ⁶ For how can I bear to see disaster fall on my people? How can I bear to see the destruction of my family?"

8:3–6 What leadership qualities does Esther exhibit?

¹¹ The king's edict granted the Jews in every city the right to assemble and protect themselves; to destroy, kill and annihilate the armed men of any nationality or province who might attack them.

8:11 Is there a sense that God has brought good from Haman's evil intents even beyond what Esther asked for?

¹² The king said to Queen Esther, "... Now what is your petition? It will be given you. What is your request? It will also be granted." ¹³ "If it pleases the king," Esther answered, "give the Jews in Susa permission to carry out this day's edict tomorrow also, and let Haman's ten sons be impaled on poles." ¹⁴ So the king commanded that this be done.

9:12–14 Esther is given yet another request from the king, and she uses her favor for the good of her people. What does this reveal about Esther's character?

DISCUSS

1. How can we relate to Esther's political climate?

2. How does Esther demonstrate leadership?

3. What does Esther teach us about responding in times of crisis?

4. How does Esther's story inspire hope?

REFLECTIONS

1. How can we relate to Esther's political climate?

Much like some rulers in our present time, the Persian government wielded great power. Policies and laws posed a threat to people of faith, who had very limited options to resist. There was great fear. To stand against the government was dangerous, as Queen Vashti's banishment from the kingdom illustrated. Officials were corrupt, and, like today, arrogant and prideful leaders sought the destruction of people of faith. Some in power hated the Jews and wanted to silence them, just as people of faith are often silenced and mocked today.

Compared to the wealth and power of the Persian kingdom, Esther was insignificant, and so she was taken from her home and family to become a concubine for the king. We too can feel powerless against systems of injustice, economic oppression, and brutal laws that seem intent on deconstructing our values, destroying our faith, and imposing rules we don't agree with.

And so, in many ways, we too live in a form of exile.

2. How does Esther demonstrate leadership?

Some argue that Esther was a secular Jew; and we can observe that God is not referenced in the book of Esther. Regardless, as people of faith, we can learn about leadership from Esther's life.

At a young age, Esther must navigate a political and existential threat to her life while living in a foreign country away from home with the lives of all her people suddenly reliant on her to rescue them. We watch her accept her elevated position fearlessly and without complaint and watch as she rises up as a savior who delivers the Jews, willingly risking her life.

Esther becomes a great leader to her people, directing them to fasting in unity. While Esther fearlessly takes a bold risk for her people, she also displays patience and calm under tremendous pressure. The king repeatedly offers to grant her a request, but Esther delays, waiting until the time is right. Throughout the story, she is willing to accept and wisely obeys Mordecai's counsel. When she is under threat, Esther demonstrates humility by fasting and, we might assume, trusts and depends on God for direction and the outcome.

We are all influencers to someone. We are all called to lead. Others are looking to us for leadership, especially during times of duress. Spiritual lives and perhaps even physical lives are at stake. Is our compassion for those who face injustice so great that we are willing to stand up against those who oppose the people of God? Will our love for people drive us to intercede on their behalf?

3. What does Esther teach us about responding in times of crisis?

The first part of Esther's response is to empathize and identify with her people. To have empathy requires us to respond to suffering. To come alongside those who are suffering. To offer a ministry of presence. Such a response is sometimes the most difficult. It demands authenticity, an investment of time, and the gift of listening. It beckons us to have an affinity with God such that those around us become aware of the presence of the Holy Spirit within us.

Next, Esther instructs the community to gather together and to fast. Rather than dwell in the state of individual mourning and fear, the people are entreated to come together as a community. When even one person in our community is hurting or in crisis, we can rally as a community and together bear the burden of the crisis. Unified, we can earnestly call upon God and expect God to respond.

Finally, Esther acts. There is no clear evidence that Esther would have died with her people—her Jewish identity was not known to Haman—nevertheless, she understands the crisis and responds. We might often be tempted to ignore suffering that doesn't impact us personally. We might reason that we can't make a difference, particularly if acting requires us to work against a system that is domineering and antagonistic against us.

In those moments, let us remember that God is able to use whatever resources and skills we have. A willing heart is all God requires to work through us. Can we take the bold step to simply offer ourselves to God as instruments of salvation? If so, let's do so—and then wait with expectation for what God will do through us!

4. How does Esther's story inspire hope?

In a time of social-political unrest, when hatred brews against people of faith, God raises up Esther from an obscure Jewish girl in exile to the office of queen in the most powerful nation on earth and accomplishes great salvation for many people. In the middle of Esther's story, God publicly exalts Mordecai before his enemy. By the end of the story, Haman's property is given to Esther, Mordecai is elevated to the highest government level in Persia, and the enemies of the Jews are eliminated.

What a powerful illustration of God's ability to turn around a situation—to humiliate the proud and exalt the humble! It shows us how God is more than able to thwart every plan conceived against us. That God is able to turn mourning to dancing, fear to joy. That God carries us from bondage to freedom, from the grasp of death to abundant life in Christ Jesus.

Just like Esther is enabled by God to overcome every disadvantage and limitation, so too we who are in Christ are called to be overcomers. God promises to take the brokenness of our past and give us new life. Even in exile, God is present and at work.

PRAYER

LORD,

When we pray to You, hear us
When we are in distress, see us
When we ask You for deliverance, respond to us
When we seek You, draw close to us

When we are held captive, set us free
When we are wronged, teach us to forgive
When we are broken, be our healer
When we feel alone, be present with us

When we are anxious, bring peace to our souls
When we are so busy, be our rest
When we get discouraged, fill us with joy
At all times, give us the courage to put our trust in You

Amen.

Mary, Mother of Jesus
LUKE 1

What opportunities do you have to "be" Christ to others?

BACKGROUND

The background for the story of Mary is provided in the first verses of Luke's Gospel:

> Many have undertaken to draw up an account of the things that have been fulfilled among us, just as they were handed down to us by those who from the first were eyewitnesses and servants of the word. With this in mind, since I myself have carefully investigated everything from the beginning, I too decided to write an orderly account for you, most excellent Theophilus, so that you may know the certainty of the things you have been taught. (Luke 1:1–4)

Luke's aim is to present an accurate history. It follows, then, that Luke wants us to consider the supernatural elements surrounding the story of Mary that we are about to read—the angel appearing and the virgin birth—as true.

Luke says that his sources are "eyewitnesses and servants of the word." How then does Luke know about Mary's personal encounter with the angel? We can assume that Mary's testimony is the source of this marvelous narrative. This is indeed Mary's story!

LUKE

1 ²⁶ In the sixth month of Elizabeth's pregnancy, God sent the angel Gabriel to Nazareth, a town in Galilee, ²⁷ to a virgin pledged to be married to a man named Joseph, a descendant of David. The virgin's name was Mary. ²⁸ The angel went to her and said, "Greetings, you who are highly favored! The Lord is with you."

²⁹ Mary was greatly troubled at his words and wondered what kind of greeting this might be. ³⁰ But the angel said to her, "Do not be afraid, Mary; you have found favor with God. ³¹ You will conceive and give birth to a son, and you are to call him Jesus. ³² He will be great and will be called the Son of the Most High. The Lord God will give him the throne of his father David, ³³ and he will reign over Jacob's descendants forever; his kingdom will never end."

³⁴ "How will this be," Mary asked the angel, "since I am a virgin?"

EXPLORE

1:26–28 Luke sets this story of Mary within the immediate context of Elizabeth's miraculous pregnancy, and the same angel, Gabriel, who appears to Elizabeth's husband to announce the coming of their child now visits Mary. How does this prepare the reader for Mary's even greater miraculous story?

How does "The Lord is with you" have special meaning for Mary?

1:29–33 Why would Mary be troubled or afraid at the words of the angel ("You who are highly favored! The Lord is with you")?

The angel states again that Mary is favored— that God has extended grace to Mary. Importantly, this is before she conceives her son. What does this tell us about being favored by God?

1:34 The angel's announcement is spectacular in many aspects, but Mary makes only one objection, and it is related to herself. What does this say about Mary's faith?

35 The angel answered, "The Holy Spirit will come on you, and the power of the Most High will overshadow you. So the holy one to be born will be called the Son of God. 36 Even Elizabeth your relative is going to have a child in her old age, and she who was said to be unable to conceive is in her sixth month. 37 For no word from God will ever fail."

38 "I am the Lord's servant," Mary answered. "May your word to me be fulfilled." Then the angel left her.

1:35–37 What does the response of the angel tell us about how God's work is accomplished?

1:38 In what ways has Mary demonstrated that she is the Lord's servant?

How will the mission to bear the Christ child require Mary to continue to submit to God's will?

What are the implications of Mary's obedience for all of humanity?

39 At that time Mary got ready and hurried to a town in the hill country of Judea, 40 where she entered Zechariah's home and greeted Elizabeth. 41 When Elizabeth heard Mary's greeting, the baby leaped in her womb, and Elizabeth was filled with the Holy Spirit. 42 In a loud voice she exclaimed: "Blessed are you among women, and blessed is the child you will bear! 43 But why am I so favored, that the mother of my Lord should come to me? 44 As soon as the sound of your greeting reached my ears, the baby in my womb leaped for joy. 45 Blessed is she who has believed that the Lord would fulfill his promises to her!"

46 And Mary said:
"My soul glorifies the Lord
47 and my spirit rejoices in God my Savior,
48 for he has been mindful
   of the humble state of his servant.
From now on all generations will call me
   blessed,
49 for the Mighty One has done great
   things for me—
   holy is his name.
50 His mercy extends to those who fear him,
   from generation to generation.

1:39–45 In response to the angel, Mary immediately goes to be with Elizabeth for three months. Why would Mary desire the companionship of Elizabeth during the first months of pregnancy?

How does Elizabeth's response confirm the words of the angel?

1:46–50 What does Mary teach us about God in this first half of her testimonial sermon?

51 He has performed mighty deeds with his
    arm;
      he has scattered those who are proud in
      their inmost thoughts.
52 He has brought down rulers from their
    thrones
      but has lifted up the humble.
53 He has filled the hungry with good things
      but has sent the rich away empty.
54 He has helped his servant Israel,
      remembering to be merciful
55 to Abraham and his descendants forever,
      just as he promised our ancestors."

1:51–55 The Greek tense of these verses indicates that God's past work is not finished or complete; God's work is timeless. As such, how does Mary provide prophetic insight into what is about to occur through Jesus's ministry?

Similarly, how does Mary's speech foretell what Jesus accomplishes through His death and resurrection?

God's mercy is for all who fear Him (verse 50), but how might the poor be specially positioned to turn to God (verse 53)?

[Several other passages refer to Mary, in addition to the birth narrative in Matthew.]

Matthew 13 [54] Coming to his hometown, he began teaching the people in their synagogue, and they were amazed. "Where did this man get this wisdom and these miraculous powers?" they asked. [55] "Isn't this the carpenter's son? Isn't his mother's name Mary, and aren't his brothers James, Joseph, Simon and Judas? [56] Aren't all his sisters with us? Where then did this man get all these things?" [57] And they took offense at him. But Jesus said to them, "A prophet is not without honor except in his own town and in his own home." [58] And he did not do many miracles there because of their lack of faith.

Matt. 13:54–58 Little is expected of Mary by the community—the people don't associate her with wisdom or the miraculous. How does this contrast with the expectation that Luke creates in our earlier narrative about Mary?

Do you think it is possible that Mary's hometown had not heard of her encounter with the angel and her supernatural pregnancy? Or, do they simply lack the faith to believe what they've heard?

Luke 11 [27] As Jesus was [teaching], a woman in the crowd called out, "Blessed is the mother who gave you birth and nursed you." [28] He replied, "Blessed rather are those who hear the word of God and obey it."

Luke 11:27–28 Mary is declared blessed numerous times by Luke. How does Jesus include others in the great blessedness that was upon Mary?

Could Jesus's claim that "those who hear the word of God and obey it" are blessed be applied to us?

John 2 ² Jesus and his disciples had also been invited to the wedding. ³ When the wine was gone, Jesus' mother said to him, "They have no more wine." ⁴ "Woman, why do you involve me?" Jesus replied. "My hour has not yet come." ⁵ His mother said to the servants, "Do whatever he tells you." [Jesus then proceeded to turn water in jugs into wine.]

John 2:2–5 This passage presents the first miracle of Jesus, and it is Mary who prompts Jesus to begin His ministry. What does this say about Mary's important role in the ministry of Jesus?

What does Mary believe about who Jesus is and what Jesus is able to do?

Mary says, "Do whatever he tells you"—how is this a prophetic instruction for all who follow Christ, not just the servants?

John 19 ²⁵ Near the cross of Jesus stood his mother, his mother's sister, Mary the wife of Clopas, and Mary Magdalene. ²⁶ When Jesus saw his mother there, and the disciple whom he loved standing nearby, he said to her, "Woman, here is your son," ²⁷ and to the disciple, "Here is your mother." From that time on, this disciple took her into his home ... ³⁰ Jesus said, "It is finished." With that, he bowed his head and gave up his spirit.

John 19:25–30 Is it significant that Mary is central to this last moment before Jesus dies?

What can we surmise about Mary's situation given that Jesus arranges for Mary to be under John's care?

[Luke continues his history in the book of Acts. He tells us that 40 days after Jesus rose from the grave to life, Jesus ascended to heaven.] **Acts 1** ¹² Then the apostles returned to Jerusalem from the hill called the Mount of Olives, a Sabbath day's walk from the city. ¹³ When they arrived, they went upstairs to the room where they were staying. Those present were Peter, John, James and Andrew; Philip and Thomas, Bartholomew and Matthew; James son of Alphaeus and Simon the Zealot, and Judas son of James. ¹⁴ They all joined together constantly in prayer, along with the women and Mary the mother of Jesus, and with his brothers.

Acts 1:12–14 This is an important reference to Mary. Who is Mary named alongside?

What does this reference indicate about Mary's status among the followers of Jesus?

At this point, has Mary completed her mission from God spoken through Gabriel to bear the son of Christ?

What can we infer about Mary's ongoing role and impact on the Early Church in the days after Jesus ascended?

DISCUSS

1. What can we learn about friendship through Mary and her relationship with Elizabeth and other women?

2. How is Mary central to God's plan of salvation for humanity?

3. How does Mary demonstrate a lifelong commitment to God's calling?

4. How can we be full of grace and favor?

REFLECTIONS

1. What can we learn about friendship through Mary and her relationship with Elizabeth and other women?

After Mary's encounter with the angel, Mary's instinct is to go to the home of Elizabeth. Mary chooses to stay with a woman who is full of faith and associated with the Holy Spirit and the miraculous power of God. We too are wise to surround ourselves with women who are filled with the Holy Spirit and whose lives reflect the work of God. Elizabeth's greeting must have profoundly encouraged Mary and affirmed the angel's message. How important it is to have people in our lives whose words are life-giving and who affirm us in the LORD, friends who rejoice merely to be in our presence!

Mary chooses to be with a woman who has just gone through similar circumstances. Their friendship and mutual support remind us that we do not need to journey through the trials of life alone and that we can pray for God to bring people into our lives who understand what we are going through and support us.

Mary is found in the company of other women at the cross when Jesus is dying and in the upper room after Jesus leaves earth. In what must be the most heartbreaking moment of Mary's life, and later as she strives to serve Jesus even after He's gone, Mary wisely chooses to be surrounded by community. Certainly, such friends are hard to come by. Let us pray for friendships during every situation we go through, and let's look for ways we can encourage and support others on their life journeys.

2. How is Mary central to God's plan of salvation for humanity?

God chose to bring Jesus into the world in human form through the womb of a woman. To this end, the angel did not *ask* Mary to bear a child—the angel *told* Mary what was about to happen. Mary's willingness to be used by God to birth Jesus enables God's plan to be fulfilled. Mary is with Jesus from the first moment of His life on earth and responsible for training Him in God's ways as a young child. Luke describes the responses Jesus received at the tender age of 12: "Everyone who heard him was amazed at his understanding and his answers" (2:47). This is in part a reflection of His upbringing. That Jesus is at the temple without His parents for three days and unafraid shows the confidence His mother instilled in Him.

Mary is present at the first miracle of Jesus. She indicates that Jesus should act. Although Jesus insists "My hour has not yet come," Mary is confident that the time *has* come. Her belief that Jesus could perform a miracle and that Jesus cared about the servants' embarrassing situation propels Jesus to move forward to do "the first of the signs through which he revealed his glory."

How can we participate in God's plan of salvation for humanity? God will not call any of us to literally bear the Son of God, but are we willing to answer God's call to bear Christ every day in our words and actions? Will we bear Christ to those who don't know Him?

In part, to bear Christ is to embody Christ—to carry Christ everywhere we go, to show others that "the Spirit of him who raised Jesus from the dead is living in you" (Rom 8:11), and to willingly and openly share the hope we have in Christ.

Will we bear Christ with joy, with praise, with thanksgiving? Can we, like Mary, testify that God has done great things for us?

3. How does Mary demonstrate a lifelong commitment to God's calling?

God's calling for each of us is to accept the salvation of Jesus Christ and then to participate in the redemptive work of God on earth—to point others to Christ.

Mary points Luke's audience to Jesus through her prophetic speech. Just as God did mighty deeds for Mary, so Jesus would perform mighty deeds for many; Jesus would extend mercy to all who fear and follow Him; He would upset the political world by revealing that true power is not found in a person on a throne but is in the Holy Spirit residing within the one who follows God. Mary points to the humble nature of Jesus and His care for those in need. Mary reminds us of the promise made to Abraham and his descendants—a promise ultimately fulfilled in Jesus. Does this give us confidence to rely on all the promises of God?

Mary participates in the redemptive work of Jesus at the wedding. Mary encourages Jesus to take note of the needs of the servants and to respond. Her speech to the servants also points to Christ— "Do whatever he tells you." These words apply to all who are servants of Jesus. We too can obey Mary's instruction in the expectation that we will see the miraculous acts of Jesus and even be part of God's miracles.

As a witness to the risen Christ, Mary testifies to the resurrection. Remarkably, even after Jesus ascends to heaven, Mary continues to do God's work, waiting for the Holy Spirit alongside the apostles. As favored by God as Mary is, she still waits for even more of what God has for her. By the time of the ascension, Mary's mission to bring Christ into the world is complete. But she is committed to the lifelong mission of bringing Jesus to all the world, and so she continues to spread the salvation message of Jesus.

Like Mary, will we testify to the great things God has done for us? Will we follow Mary's example to boldly point others to obey and follow Jesus? Will we be witnesses that Christ has risen and share the message of salvation? Will we exhibit the same lifelong commitment to serving God?

God has called all of us to participate in the redemptive work of God. And whatever God calls us to do, God will accomplish through us! As the angel told Mary, "no word from God will ever fail."

4. How can we be full of grace and favor?

Mary is a humble recipient of God's mercy. She willingly accepts God's mission. Mary is blessed—though God's calling to bear the Son of God would lead to the heartache of witnessing her son being ridiculed, rejected, mocked, and finally, crucified. And the angel expands on Mary's favor with God by telling her, "The Holy Spirit will come on you, and the power of the Most High will overshadow you."

This tells us that being full of grace and favor is related to humility and a willingness to respond to God's call. It means we are blessed by God even when we face trials and hardship as we follow God's calling on our lives. To be full of God's grace is to be filled with the Holy Spirit! It is to go in the power of the Most High!

We too can be full of God's grace and favor! We can come to God humbly and accept the offer of God's mercy. We can respond to God with obedience whenever the Holy Spirit prompts us to "bear" Christ to others. We can reflect on all the mighty things God has done for us and then share our testimony about God's greatness everywhere we go.

MARINA HOFMAN

PRAYER

LORD,

You go before us and prepare our way
You are the God of the impossible
You confirm Your word; You do not fail to do what You promise

We are favored! We are cherished!
We belong to the Most High King!
We are marked by God and filled with the Holy Spirit!

With humility, we receive Your mercy
Give us a willing heart to respond to Your calling
May we experience Your mighty works and declare them

May no weapon formed against us prosper
May those who rise up against us be brought low
The LORD saves, the LORD redeems, the LORD is our victory

Praise the name of the LORD!

Amen.

BIOGRAPHY AND TESTIMONY

Marina Hofman, PhD, is an interdisciplinary scholar who writes and speaks on biblical studies, trauma, education, ministry, and ethics. Female characters in the Bible is her favorite field! She has taught in Canada, the United States, Colombia (South America), and The Gambia (West Africa). Presently, Marina is a faculty member at Palm Beach Atlantic University in South Florida.

Her national awards include the Emerging Old Testament Scholar award by the Institute of Biblical Research at the Society of Biblical Literature and Best Paper by the Canadian-American Evangelical Theological Association. A native of Canada, she earned a PhD in theology at the University of Toronto, along with a post-doctorate certificate in teaching higher education, as well as an MA from McMaster University and a BA from Tyndale University College.

Marina has shared her testimony to people around the world. She is grateful every day for God's miraculous healing, her family, and the hope she has in Christ!

> In 2014, my husband and I were in a head-on vehicle collision north of Toronto, Ontario, on Highway 69. The impact was equal to a total speed of about 125 miles per hour. It was a fatal crash for the driver who hit us, and in that moment, we did not know if we would survive.
>
> I incurred four lacerations to my bowels and was nearly dead by the time I reached the hospital. But God preserved my life. At the crash site, within seconds, I was surrounded by emergency workers who prevented me from moving, thus saving my life. A top surgeon was waiting for me at the hospital when I arrived and realized that there was no time for tests to determine my injuries. She immediately administered life-saving surgery by examining all of my organs by hand, and then another top surgeon repaired the damaged areas. Again, my life was saved.

The next urgent need was to make sure I did not lose hope and give up on life as the horror of what had happened gradually dawned on me. When I woke up after surgery, my husband's fate was still unsure, and I felt completely disoriented—hardly able to communicate and suffering chronic memory loss. Again, God was present. For the whole first week of my recovery, a team of truly tender-hearted ICU nurses did not leave my side, even for a moment.

Eventually, I was told I had experienced significant physical injuries and suffered a minor brain injury. In the days that followed, I was diagnosed with severe posttraumatic stress disorder, among other emotional and mental incapacities.

Although my mental state was poor and I was constantly anxious, we discovered that it could have been much worse. In the effort to reconstruct how the crash occurred, a detective interviewed my husband. The detective shared that the computer program his department uses could not produce a scenario where my husband survived. My husband responded that at the last moment, when the brakes disengaged and all was lost, he threw his body over the caddy and leaned over the passenger's side as far as he could so that his body would protect me from any projectile or broken glass. He had held my head back against the headrest to minimize my whiplash. This act not only saved me from a much worse brain injury but also saved his own life from being crushed by the engine that was pushed upward into his driver's seat.

Our road to recovery has been long. I needed to learn how to overcome depression, anxiety, and hyper attentiveness. Regaining my cognitive functions was a slow process and required me to completely reorder my life. I had to accept that the memories of my past might never return.

Most painful of all was the diagnosis that I would not be able to have children. If I did get pregnant, I was told, it would be very painful and risky.

But God's ways are beyond our imagination. God takes the most impossible situation and turns it for good. God takes the broken pieces of our lives and puts us back together. God picks us up when we can't walk any further. When all seems lost, God redeems our life and fills us with joy.

Today, my life is a testimony that with God all things are possible.

My husband and I live in South Florida, where our injuries continue to heal. By God's grace, we have a wonderful little daughter, Willow Grace Hannah, who is the daily delight of our lives. Despite aches and pains—ongoing reminders of how far God has brought us and what could have happened that fateful day—we have a joyful life, with many laughs and daily dance parties in our living room, often to Christmas music.

We worship and serve at Christ Fellowship Gardens Campus, where we are blessed with genuine community and rest for our souls.

To connect with Marina, book a speaking engagement, and learn more about Marina's upcoming publications, visit:

WWW.WOMENINTHEBIBLE.INFO

Visit www.WomenInTheBible.info

to access the video series for this book and to connect with Marina Hofman.

Visit www.CastleQuayBooks.com

for more titles like this one, including Bible studies, devotionals, and inspiration.

CASTLE QUAY BOOKS

CPSIA information can be obtained
at www.ICGtesting.com
Printed in the USA
LVHW021945130622
721151LV00005B/383